DINOWORLD
Brachiosaurus

DAVID UNWIN

Kingfisher

NEW YORK

CONTENTS

INTRODUCTION

Who can imagine standing next to *Brachiosaurus*, its head appearing to disappear into the clouds! Well, perhaps not the clouds, but at 13 feet (4 m) above the ground, I'd rather watch *Brachiosaurus* out of a third-floor window. This kind of dinosaur, one of more than one hundred species of sauropods (meaning "reptile feet"), would have taken your breath away, no matter which way you looked at them. *Brachiosaurus* was some 80 feet (25 m) long and weighed at least 50 tons, about as heavy as ten elephants. And there were sauropods who were longer and heavier still. At present, the record appears to be an animal named *Seismosaurus* ("Earth-shaking reptile"), which reached almost 130 feet (40 m) in length and may have weighed as much as 75 tons.

Such sizable land-living creatures would have had an enormous appetite. Just how much would it take to feed a *Brachiosaurus*? For such a large animal, the mouth is rather small and there are no chewing teeth to chomp up the leaves and branches before they are swallowed. Stomach stones helped remedy this funny situation, but even so, these sauropods must have spent all day, and most of the night, feeding on the leaves of tall trees, much as giraffes do today. It must have taken huge amounts of vegetation to keep a sauropod's stomach from rumbling. But what's this about tall trees? Didn't *Brachiosaurus* and its relatives live in lakes and swamps? Didn't they need to support their heavy bulk by buoying themselves up in deep water? In a word: "No." We now know that animals like *Brachiosaurus* were no more stuck in the water than are animals like rhinoceroses today. These giant dinosaurs were thorough-going land animals. You are going to read about some of the most spectacular creatures ever to have lived on land. With their small heads, long tails, and enormous bodies, they are like fantasy animals, too big to have really existed—only they did exist! Turn the page and you'll be able to begin the sauropod adventure.

David B. Weishampel
Associate
Professor
Johns Hopkins
University

A DINOSAUR TIMELINE

One of the best known periods in the history of the dinosaurs is the late Jurassic. Dinosaurs had already been around for over 60 million years, and they now completely dominated life on land. The sauropods, such as *Brachiosaurus*, *Dicraeosaurus*, and *Camarasaurus*, were at the height of their reign as the main plant-eating dinosaurs. They lived alongside other herbivores, such as *Stegosaurus*, *Dryosaurus*, and *Camptosaurus*, whose descendants, the iguanodontids and hadrosaurids, would largely replace the sauropods in the Cretaceous period.

6 *Dicraeosaurus*

2 *Camptosaurus*

5 *Dryosaurus*

▶ The Jurassic was the middle period of the Mesozoic era, and lasted from about 205 million to 145 million years ago. Many different kinds of dinosaur appeared during the Jurassic, including feathered ones, which gave rise to birds.

4 *Elaphrosaurus*

	LATE TRIASSIC			JURASSIC		
				Early		Middle
Millions of Years Ago						
230	220	210	200	190	180	170	160

▼ The late Jurassic earth shook as herds of *Dicraeosaurus* and *Brachiosaurus* tramped along in search of plant fodder. These moving mountains of flesh were trailed by meat-eating ceratosaurs, hoping to pick off the young or the weak. Many herbivores developed defensive techniques. While sauropods relied on sheer size, *Stegosaurus* armed itself with long spikes, and *Dryosaurus* evolved long, powerful, high-speed legs.

1 *Brachiosaurus*

3 *Ceratosaurus*

CRETACEOUS

Early

Late

145   130   110   100   95   90   80   70 65

150 MILLION YEARS AGO

The face of the Earth is continually changing as the continents slowly drift apart to form new oceans, or collide with each other to produce mountain chains. Early in the Dinosaur Age, the continents were massed together in a single supercontinent called Pangaea. By the late Jurassic, Pangaea had broken up into Laurasia in the north, and Gondwanaland in the south.

▼ In the late Jurassic, rising sea levels had drowned much of Europe and separated Asia from the other continents. However, Africa and North America, were joined part of the time, and many of the same dinosaurs were found on both continents.

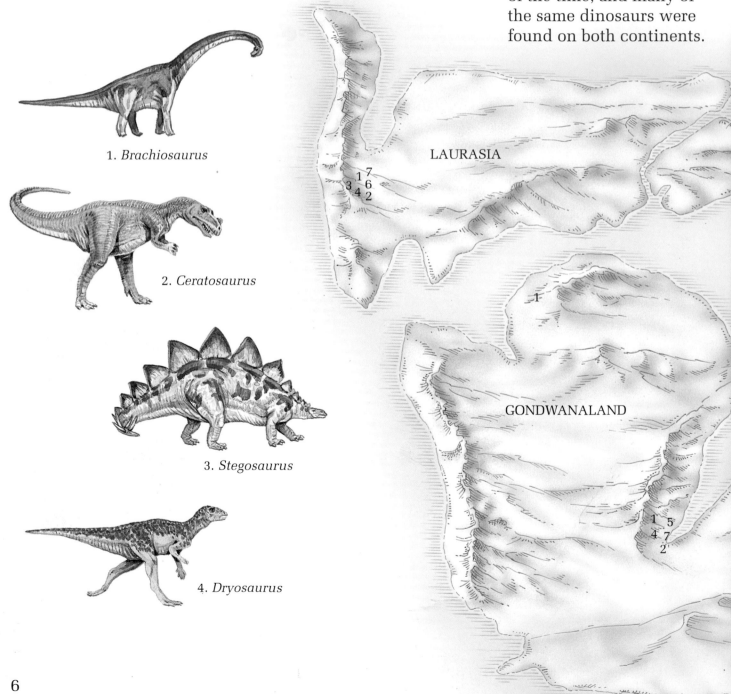

1. *Brachiosaurus*

2. *Ceratosaurus*

3. *Stegosaurus*

4. *Dryosaurus*

LAURASIA

GONDWANALAND

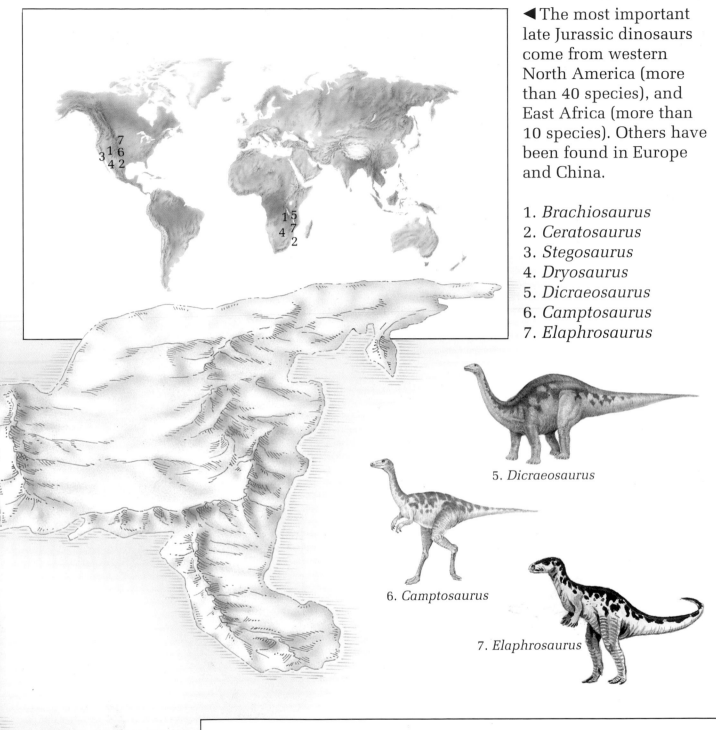

◄ The most important late Jurassic dinosaurs come from western North America (more than 40 species), and East Africa (more than 10 species). Others have been found in Europe and China.

1. *Brachiosaurus*
2. *Ceratosaurus*
3. *Stegosaurus*
4. *Dryosaurus*
5. *Dicraeosaurus*
6. *Camptosaurus*
7. *Elaphrosaurus*

5. *Dicraeosaurus*

6. *Camptosaurus*

7. *Elaphrosaurus*

PERIOD	**CONTINENTS**	**CLIMATE**
Late Jurassic 157–145 million years ago	Two large continents separated by the proto-Atlantic in the west and the ocean Tethys in the east.	Very mild and warm even at high latitudes. Most land areas experienced moist conditions and the few desert areas were very small.

PREHISTORIC TENDAGURU

Brachiosaurus lived in an area that paleontologists call Tendaguru, in what is now East Africa, on a flat coastal plain covered with conifer forests and areas of more open vegetation. Shallow rivers flowed across the plain, feeding through marshy deltas into a shallow sea, which lay to the east. Occasionally this sea flooded the area, forcing the dinosaurs to move elsewhere for food.

▼ A herd of *Brachiosaurus* use their long necks to harvest the upper branches of Tendaguru conifers.

▼ A large, primitive lacewing unfolds its paired wings before it lifts off into the Jurassic sky.

▶ *Kentrosaurus* was a tanklike, plant-eating dinosaur, that had plates and spines for armor. Here, it is plodding along in search of low-growing vegetation to eat. Its plates and spines protected it from small predators.

▲ Conifers and ferns provided most of the ground cover, mixed with cycads and ginkgoes.

▲ These massive
legs belong to a
Brachiosaurus, one
of the largest and
tallest dinosaurs.

▲ Small pterosaurs
hunt for insects, stirred
up by *Brachiosaurus* as it
lumbers through the
undergrowth.

▲ *Dryosaurus*, a fast-
moving herbivore,
keeps a lookout for
predators.

THE TENDAGURU COMMUNITIES

In Tendaguru, two different communities lived side by side; one on the land and one in the sea. Dinosaurs dominated the land community. Plants supported the many herbivorous dinosaurs, which were eaten by carnivorous dinosaurs. Plants also provided food and shelter for insects, the main diet of lizards and pterosaurs. Out in the shallow, warm sea, small fish were preyed upon by sharks, marine reptiles, and fish-eating pterosaurs.

Pterosaurs

Skimming over the surface of the sea, the pterosaur *Rhamphorhynchus* used its long, sharp, pointed beak to scoop up fish.

Sharks

Early sharks such as *Hybodus* were common in Jurassic seas, polishing off the dead, the dying, and the unwary.

Insects

Most Jurassic insects fed on plants. Some insects tackled larger animals, living as parasites on dinosaur skin or by sucking dinosaur blood.

Cockroach

Mayfly

Water boatman

Water scorpion

Dragonfly

Pterosaurs

With powerful beats of its long wings, *Anurognathus* pursued insects, such as lacewings, engulfing them in its wide open jaws.

Lizards

Sphenodontids were small lizardlike reptiles that fed on plants or insects. A single species, the Tuatara, still lives in parts of New Zealand.

Sea reptiles

Pleurosaurus, and many other reptiles, took to a life in the seas, evolving long streamlined bodies, and flipperlike fore and hind limbs.

Fish

Many fish lived in the coral reefs off the Tendaguru coast. *Gyrodus* broke open coral with rows of crushing teeth, in order to feed on polyps.

11

ENEMIES AND COMPETITORS

Careful studies of their fossil remains show that, like modern animals, each of the Tendaguru dinosaurs lived in its own particular way. *Brachiosaurus* and the other sauropods played the role of heavyweight herbivores, like elephants and buffaloes. *Kentrosaurus* looks like a Jurassic rhinoceros, while, at a distance, herds of *Dryosaurus* might easily be mistaken for kangaroos. Their enemies were predators such as *Ceratosaurus*, much larger and more dangerous than modern lions, and the small high-speed killer, *Elaphrosaurus*, which may have hunted in packs as jackals do today. Instead of birds, the air was filled with pterosaurs.

▶ Adult brachiosaurs were too large to deal with. But, if a young animal became separated from the herd, *Ceratosaurus* pounced, killing its victim with a few swift bites. A few tons of fresh brachiosaur lasted for days!

Kentrosaurus

KEN-tro-SAW-rus
"SPIKY REPTILE"
17 FT. (5 M) LONG

Kentrosaurus was a stegosaur, with plates and sharp, pointed spines running down its back.

Ceratosaurus

SER-a-toe-SAW-rus
"HORNED REPTILE"
20 FT. (6 M) LONG

Only great size or
great speed could
save you from this
Jurassic terminator
that was armed with
bladelike teeth.

DOWN IN THE UNDERGROWTH

Not all dinosaurs were giants. *Dryosaurus* was a small, lightly built animal. The short forelimbs and five-fingered hands were used to scratch up roots or tear up vegetation. Using a long stiffened tail to balance on its powerful hind limbs, this was a fast and agile dinosaur, capable of outrunning anything, except perhaps *Elaphrosaurus*. Dryosaurs were also very efficient feeders, nipping off leaves or fronds with their bony beaks, storing them in cheek pouches, and then chopping them up with sharp, chisellike teeth.

> ### *Dryosaurus*
>
> DRY-o-SAW-rus
> "OAK REPTILE"
> 13 FT. (4 M) LONG
>
> The herd of *Dryosaurus* are keeping a wary eye on the *Elaphrosaurus* pack, now feasting on their sibling.

Elaphrosaurus

ee-LAF-roe-
SAW-rus
"LIGHTWEIGHT
REPTILE"
11.6 FT. (3.5 M)
LONG

A fast-moving and
dangerous predator,
which probably
hunted in packs.

15

THE TALLEST DINOSAUR?

Capable of peering over a three-story house, *Brachiosaurus* was one of the tallest animals ever found. In some ways it was like other sauropod dinosaurs: a giant size, with a small head, a long neck, and a long tail. The limbs were stout and pillarlike, in order to support the enormous body weight—though some of the load was reduced by hollow, air-filled spaces in the neck bones. Unlike most sauropods, where the neck was held level, *Brachiosaurus* could lift its neck up almost upright. As the forelimbs were much longer than the hind limbs, this gave *Brachiosaurus* an enormous reach, like that of the giraffe, only much higher.

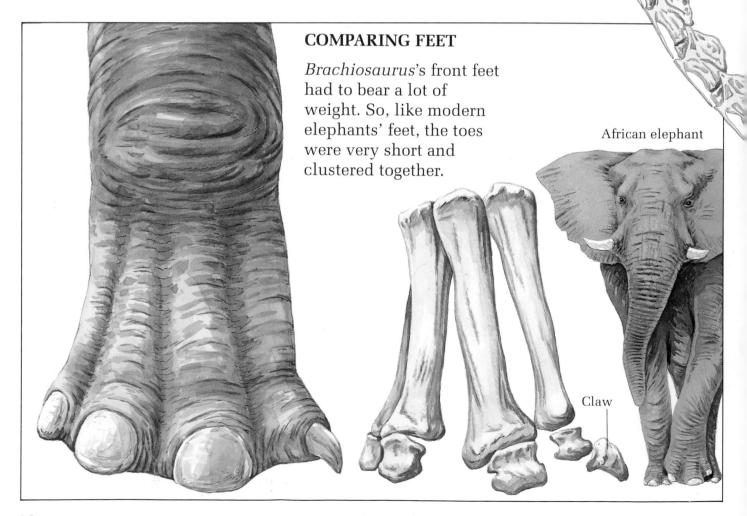

COMPARING FEET

Brachiosaurus's front feet had to bear a lot of weight. So, like modern elephants' feet, the toes were very short and clustered together.

African elephant

Claw

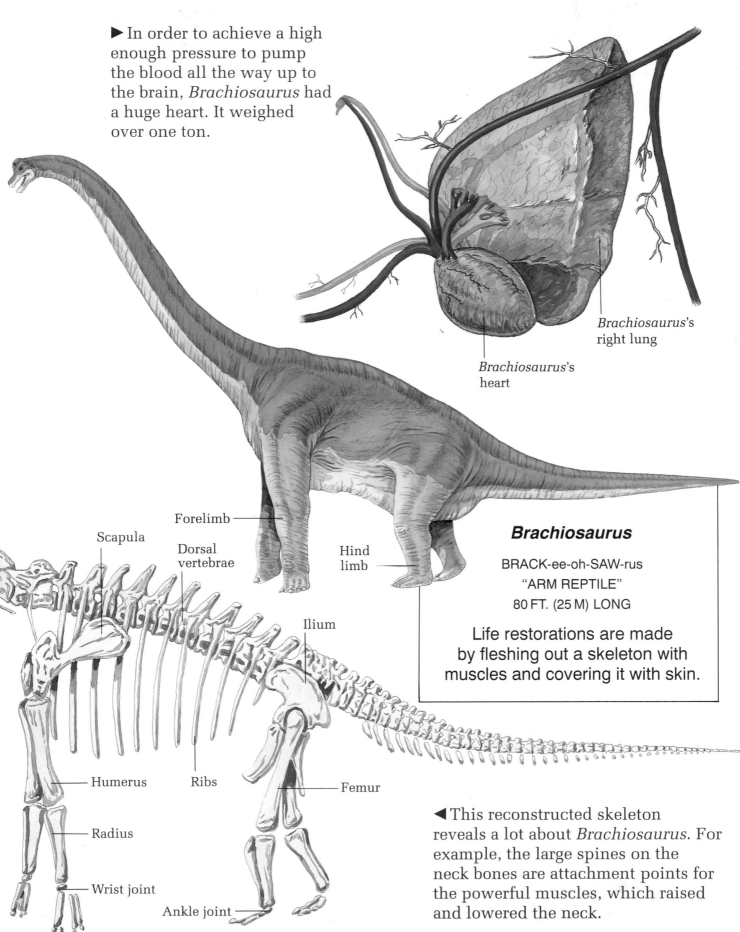

▶ In order to achieve a high enough pressure to pump the blood all the way up to the brain, *Brachiosaurus* had a huge heart. It weighed over one ton.

Brachiosaurus's right lung

Brachiosaurus's heart

Brachiosaurus

BRACK-ee-oh-SAW-rus
"ARM REPTILE"
80 FT. (25 M) LONG

Life restorations are made by fleshing out a skeleton with muscles and covering it with skin.

Scapula

Forelimb

Dorsal vertebrae

Hind limb

Ilium

Humerus

Ribs

Femur

Radius

Wrist joint

Ankle joint

◀ This reconstructed skeleton reveals a lot about *Brachiosaurus*. For example, the large spines on the neck bones are attachment points for the powerful muscles, which raised and lowered the neck.

17

THE INCREDIBLE EATING MACHINE

All large herbivores have a problem in common—
in order to avoid starvation they have to eat
almost continuously. It was even worse for
Brachiosaurus—not only was it a gigantic size, but
all its food had to pass through a very small head.
How did it solve this difficult problem? Perhaps
Brachiosaurus had a slower lifestyle than other
living herbivores and so didn't need to eat so much.
Even so, it must have eaten between 100 and
400 pounds (50 and 200 kg) of plants a day. Feeding
almost constantly, *Brachiosaurus* used chisellike
teeth to rake vegetation into its mouth. Its food was
digested as it passed through the intestines. The
waste reemerged at the other end as large droppings.

► *Brachiosaurus*'s huge
body was almost
entirely filled with
guts. These were
yards of intestine,
and an enormous
stomach that gurgled
away with stewed
vegetation.

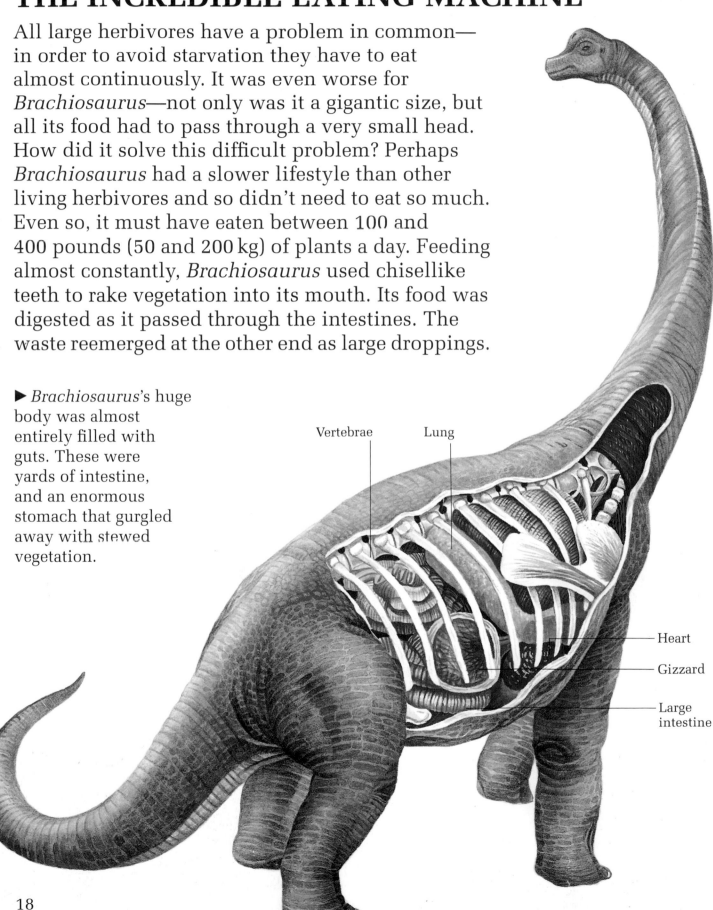

Vertebrae   Lung

Heart

Gizzard

Large
intestine

STOMACH STONES

Conifer leaves made up the bulk of *Brachiosaurus*'s diet, supplemented by cycads and ginkgoes. As some heavily worn teeth show, this was tough stuff. *Brachiosaurus* didn't chew its food, but ground it up in its gizzard, using specially swallowed stones (gastroliths).

Gastroliths

Plant food

▼ Herds of *Brachiosaurus* and *Barosaurus*, eating almost continuously, had a devastating effect on the local vegetation. The other Tendaguru herbivores fed among the undergrowth, eating those plants which the sauropods left behind. So, each animal had its own way of life and avoided direct competition with its neighbors.

HIGH

Brachiosaurus was a high browser, reaching up with its long neck to feed on the tops of trees.

MIDDLE

Barosaurus was a middle-level browser, feeding on bushes and the lower branches of conifers.

LOW

Kentrosaurus and *Dryosaurus* were low-level browsers, grazing on small plants such as ferns.

19

GENTLE GIANTS OF THE JURASSIC

Paleontologists have long puzzled over a most important question—what was *Brachiosaurus*'s way of life? Living animals don't help because there is nothing like *Brachiosaurus* on Earth today. Fortunately, fossils provide us with clues as to how extinct animals lived. Details of the teeth show what kinds of foods were eaten. The shape of the skull and the size of the eyes and nostrils, show how important the senses were. How animals walked is revealed by the size and shape of the limb bones. These kinds of evidence give us an accurate picture of how dinosaurs lived.

▼ Perhaps *Brachiosaurus* supported its great weight by living under water, using the nostrils on top of its skull to "snorkel," and eating water plants with its simple teeth. But this can't be right, because the water pressure would have stopped *Brachiosaurus* from breathing.

◀ Perhaps *Brachiosaurus* galloped around and reared up on its hind limbs. In fact, it was too heavy to run, and wouldn't have stood on two legs in case it fell and injured itself.

▶ A slow lifestyle seems most likely. Fossil trackways show that *Brachiosaurus* ambled around at a gentle pace and, most surprisingly, probably lived in family groups.

A DINOSAUR GRAVEYARD

The fates of Tendaguru dinosaurs were many and varied. Most never became fossils because they were eaten by scavengers or decayed away. As carcasses floated down rivers and out to sea, odd bones, parts of the spine, even whole limbs, sometimes dropped away and became buried in sediment. Great concentrations of skeletons, all belonging to *Kentrosaurus* or *Dryosaurus*, have been found piled together. After the droughts that caused these mass deaths, the carcasses were heaped together by floods during the rainy season.

▼ Occasionally the big sauropods became trapped in boggy areas. The exposed parts of the body decayed away, or were carried off by scavengers, attracted by the smell of rotting flesh.

SCAVENGERS

Light enough to cross the mud without getting stuck, *Elaphrosaurus* prepares to feast on the huge carcasses of dead and dying brachiosaur.

▼ Herbivore bones with bite marks, and broken carnivore teeth, show that meat-eating dinosaurs scavenged sauropod carcasses. Other scavengers included late Jurassic crocodiles.

BRACHIOSAURUS'S RELATIVES

Sauropods survived to the end of the Dinosaur Age. But they were far less numerous in the Cretaceous period, making way for plant-eating ornithopod dinosaurs, like *Iguanodon*. *Brachiosaurus*'s own line survived into the early Cretaceous, where it is represented by an English dinosaur, *Pelorosaurus*. The most important late Cretaceous sauropods were the titanosaurs, which include some remarkable dinosaurs: *Hypselosaurus*, one of the few sauropods for which fossil eggs are known; a miniature sauropod, *Magyarosaurus*; and two armored sauropods from South America, *Titanosaurus* and *Saltasaurus*.

Saltasaurus

SALT-a-SAW-rus
"SALTA REPTILE"
40 FT. (12 M) LONG

BODY ARMOR

Saltasaurus's back and upper sides were protected by armor, consisting of large, oval bony plates, surrounded by small bony studs.

Abelisaurus

ah-BELL-i-SAW-rus
"ABEL'S REPTILE"

A recently discovered large theropod; its length is unknown.

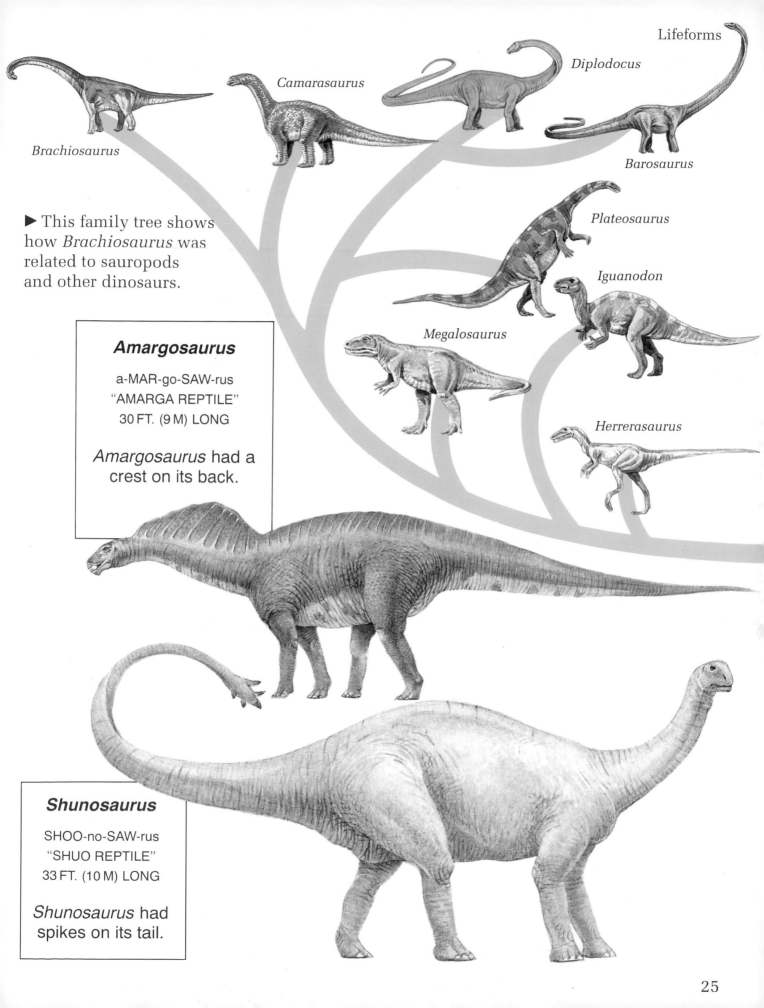

Lifeforms

Brachiosaurus

Camarasaurus

Diplodocus

Barosaurus

Plateosaurus

Iguanodon

Megalosaurus

Herrerasaurus

▶ This family tree shows how *Brachiosaurus* was related to sauropods and other dinosaurs.

Amargosaurus

a-MAR-go-SAW-rus
"AMARGA REPTILE"
30 FT. (9 M) LONG

Amargosaurus had a crest on its back.

Shunosaurus

SHOO-no-SAW-rus
"SHUO REPTILE"
33 FT. (10 M) LONG

Shunosaurus had spikes on its tail.

DINOSAUR GIANTS

Dinosaurs outperformed living animals in a number of ways, most especially in their size. *Brachiosaurus* may have weighed up to ten times more than the largest land animal, the African elephant (6 tons). However, some dinosaurs may have been twice the size of *Brachiosaurus*! How do we calculate the size of a dinosaur? With a complete dinosaur, such as *Brachiosaurus*, the height and length can be measured directly from the skeleton. Rough estimates of a dinosaur's weight can be found by measuring a model.

———*Ultrasaurus*

▼ Many groups of animals have taken advantage of being large. It is more energy efficient, and bigger animals are better able to compete for food and mates. Large size also helps to frighten off predators.

Ultrasaurus

ULL-tra-SAW-rus
"ULTRA REPTILE"
97 FT. (30 M) LONG

This brachiosaurid from the late Jurassic of Colorado, may have weighed over 150 tons.

▼ There is a maximum likely size for animals (between 100–200 tons), and it looks like sauropods reached it. However, such large size brings lots of problems. Just to keep going, these dinosaurs had to eat almost continuously. Also, because of their relatively small surface area, there was a severe risk of heat stroke. Perhaps their long necks helped to get rid of excess heat.

Seismosaurus

SIZE-mo-SAW-rus
"EARTH-SHAKING REPTILE"
130 FT. (40 M) LONG

A diplodocid from the late Jurassic of the United States. Only the spine and hips have been found.

Supersaurus

SUPER-SAW-rus
"SUPER REPTILE"
80–100 FT. (25–30 M) LONG

A diplodocid from the late Jurassic of Colorado. It may have weighed less than *Brachiosaurus*.

Supersaurus

Brachiosaurus

◄ *Brachiosaurus* had a length of about 80 feet (25 m) and a head height of 40 feet (12 m). It probably weighed at least 50 tons, although estimates of its weight vary from as little as 15, to as much as 78 tons.

DINOFACTS

Q: What sort of skin did *Brachiosaurus* have, and what color was it?

An African elephant

A: Skin is not preserved in any *Brachiosaurus*. But judging by living reptiles and other dinosaurs where skin has been found, it was probably very thick, tough, and scaly. In color, *Brachiosaurus* was probably just a fairly drab green or brown; like elephants, they were just too big to mess with, so they didn't need camouflage coloration.

Q: Could *Brachiosaurus* make any sounds?

A: Like living reptiles, *Brachiosaurus* could probably only hiss or grunt, but it might also have been able to honk or hoot by forcing air out through its partly closed nostrils.

Q: Did *Brachiosaurus* lay eggs like other dinosaurs?

A: *Brachiosaurus* eggs have never been found, but descendants of *Brachiosaurus* appear to have laid large eggs over 10 inches (25 cm) in diameter and with rough pebbly areas. When the baby hatched it weighed about 20 pounds (10 kg) and measured about 3 feet (1 m) long.

Q: How intelligent was *Brachiosaurus*?

A: Weight for weight *Brachiosaurus* has the smallest brain of almost any dinosaur, only one-hundred-thousandth of its body weight (the human brain is one-fortieth of human body weight). Evidently this huge, plant-eating plodder was no Jurassic mastermind.

The brain of *Stegosaurus*

A fossilized egg of the sauropod *Hypselosaurus* compared to a chicken's egg.

Q: Did *Brachiosaurus* live in herds?

A: Probably yes. Many trackways that seem to have been made by groups of slow-moving animals are now known. Sometimes the skeletons of many animals are found preserved together. These *Brachiosaurus* graveyards are possibly the remains of a herd that ran (or rather plodded) into some kind of natural disaster.

A giant tortoise

Q: How long did a *Brachiosaurus* live?

A: It is well known that, in general, large animals live longer than small ones; elephants reach up to 70 years of age, for example, and some large reptiles such as tortoises are known to have existed for over 150 years. *Brachiosaurus*, a gigantic reptile, probably lived for over a hundred years, and possibly much longer.

Q: Why is *Brachiosaurus* not alive today?

A: Animal species don't last that long; a few million years at most. *Brachiosaurus* probably only lasted a few million years, but its descendants carried on the line for at least another 40 million years. Eventually they too died out, perhaps because of changes in the climate or the vegetation, or perhaps from competition with other more efficient plant-eating dinosaurs such as hadrosaurs.

▲ Trackways of a sauropod and a theropod dinosaur

▼ Hadrosaurs, such as *Parasaurolophus* from North America, may have competed with Cretaceous sauropods for food.

FINDING *BRACHIOSAURUS*

As the 20th century dawned, one of the great paleontological discoveries of all time was made at Tendaguru, in Tanzania, East Africa. Between 1908 and 1912, an expedition, led by Janensch and Hennig from the Humboldt Museum in Berlin, discovered thousands of dinosaur bones, including those of *Brachiosaurus.* Conditions were very difficult. It was stiflingly hot and there was a serious risk of catching malaria. Despite this, the expedition was very successful and over 250 tons of bones were collected by teams of up to 500 excavators.

▼ Bones were encased in plaster and wrapped in grass and bamboo. Then they had to be carried 60 miles (96 kms) to the coast, to be shipped to Germany.

▶ Standing over 40 feet (12 m) high, the fully mounted specimen of *Brachiosaurus* in the Humboldt Museum, Berlin, is one of the world's largest and most spectacular dinosaur exhibits.

▲ Over 80 articulated skeletons and thousands of isolated bones were collected. The largest bones measured nearly 10 feet (3 m) long, and weighed as much as 550 pounds (250 kg).

DEATH IN THE SWAMP

All known facts about dinosaurs and their habitats have been entered in a computer program called DINO, designed by world-famous paleontologist Dr. Karl Harlow. He has linked this up to a Virtual Reality machine, with controls that allow the operators to move through the computer-generated landscapes, as though they are living dinosaurs themselves. Dr. Harlow has devised a number of "games" that will allow him to observe how dinosaurs may have behaved under certain circumstances. To this, he has added the "Random Effect"—unpredicatable circumstances caused by the presence of the player in the game. The players are his children: Buddy, a thirteen-year-old girl, who is brilliant at computer games, and Rob, her ten-year-old brother, who is mad about dinosaurs and wants to be a paleontologist. When "playing" DINO, Buddy and Rob will have to get as close to the Virtual dinosaurs as possible. They may even have to kill to survive, or become hunted themselves, and risk "death by dinosaur!"

Rob felt the familiar electronic triggers inside the Virtual Reality glove, heard the static hiss in his helmet speakers as the computer booted up the DINO program, and settled himself into the VR rig in readiness for his next adventure into the computer-generated past. He was going back 150 million years at the throw of a switch—into the humid and hostile world of the Jurassic period, where huge forests flourished and huge creatures roamed in them. This was the time of the largest land-living animals that have ever walked on Earth: the gigantic sauropods. One of the tallest among them, the height of a three-story building, was Brachiosaurus. And it was this loafing, lumbering giant that Rob was about to observe.

Rob wondered what the computer would choose for his BV or Biovehicle—the creature whose body he would "borrow" for the length of the mission. His curiosity was soon satisfied. His father spoke to him over the VR helmet speakers:

Anurognathus

"Your BV just came through, Rob. It's *Anurognathus*." Rob's heart sank. He had hoped for the fast-strutting *Elaphrosaurus*, or the sharp-fanged *Ceratosaurus*. But the pterosaur *Anurognathus*, about the size of a crow, looked like an overgrown puffin.

"That's just great, Dad," he said, unable to hide his disappointment.

"Take care, Rob, remember this is the first time you've flown."

The computer hummed more loudly as it switched to VR, and the screensaver of gliding pterosaurs faded. It was replaced with a thickly forested scene. Mist hung over high canopies of trees, a brown river threaded through a low flood plain, and far off was the metallic glint of a Jurassic sea. As Rob moved his finger controls, the horizon suddenly shifted, tilting the scene at a sickening angle. Rob caught his breath as he realized he was flying several hundred feet above the ground, and was clearly out of control. He tried more finger movements, and found himself upside down with the forest occupying the top half of the screen and the sky the lower half. He heard himself shriek as the screen tumbled and turned, and he crashed dizzily into the conifer trees.

He lost several vital seconds as he recovered his balance. Using his controls, he grasped a branch for all his worth. When he had stopped panting, he said, "That was terrific." He went through the orientation procedure, using his other hand on the menu buttons.

"The year counter reads 153 million years, and the clock 8:02 A.M. Locator reads East Africa, Tanzania. Weather is ... well, I can't tell because I'm in a thick mist, sitting at the top of a tree."

As he made his report, a sound like thunder vibrated in his helmet speakers. But he soon realized that this was no thunderstorm—it was a deep rumbling like bull elephants make, but twenty times louder. It was the noise, Rob then understood, made by a creature 10 times an elephant's size—a *Brachiosaurus*!

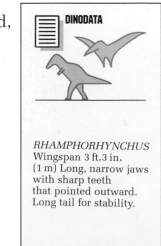

DINODATA

RHAMPHORHYNCHUS
Wingspan 3 ft. 3 in.
(1 m) Long, narrow jaws
with sharp teeth
that pointed outward.
Long tail for stability.

The head suddenly appeared out of the mist, at the level of the conifers' upper branches. Rob tried to shrink in size, as the huge head snatched a vast quantity of leaves with its mouth only a yard from where he perched, showering the ground far below with debris. The mist was rapidly clearing as the sun rose, and he could now make out the whole shape of the enormous creature. The tail, all 23 feet (7 m) of it, and as long as a derrick crane neck, scythed at the rear. Rob wondered if these were just counterbalancing movements, or a type of rearguard defense to

Rob landed clumsily upon the back of the brachiosaur.

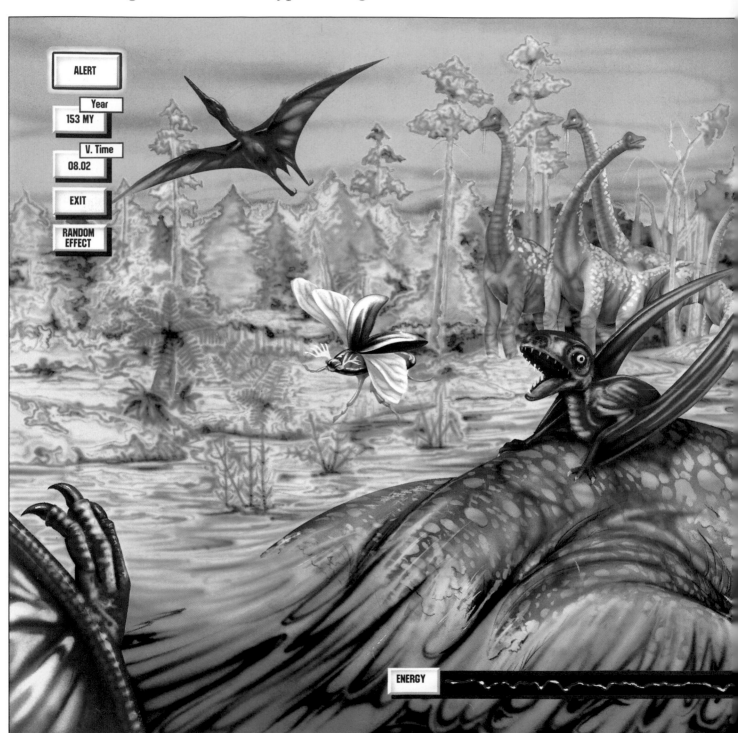

ALERT

Year
153 MY

V. Time
08.02

EXIT

RANDOM
EFFECT

ENERGY

prevent surprise attacks. Rob remembered reading somewhere that these animals may have had two brains—one in their heads, and another secondary nerve center near the tails. Perhaps the rear legs and tail were under the control of the secondary brain.

The first adult that had fed on this treetop refuge was followed by three more adults and two juveniles. Rob assumed they were making the low frequency rumbling noise to communicate with the main herd, a bit like whales do across vast ocean distances. Gently steaming, like a flotilla of ocean liners through a sea of foliage, these landbound giants left a wake of devastation as they passed onward.

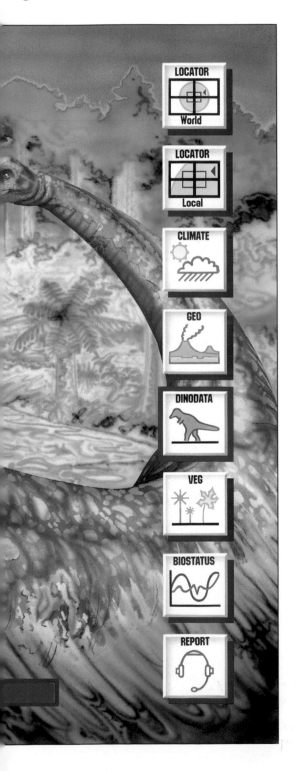

LOCATOR
World

LOCATOR
Local

CLIMATE

GEO

DINODATA

VEG

BIOSTATUS

REPORT

He knew he could not stay perched in the tree while the DINO program ran through its precious minutes. He had to make a move—and either fly safely, or fall to the ground and out, most likely, of DINO. He launched himself into the air with gentle movements of his finger controls. The screen somersaulted again, but less violently than before. He brought the horizon under control, and found to his amazement that he was gaining height as he was lifted by a thermal current of rising air. He rose above the conifers, and gained a superb view of the East African scene once more. Way below he saw the gently plodding family of brachiosaurs moving toward a group of ten or so others over to the west. It was toward these that he now began to fly.

As he moved the controls, he tumbled in the air. A whooshing noise, the flap of leathery wings, and a loud scream was all he knew about the attack from *Rhamphorhynchus*, a predatory pterosaur. It banked in the air for another attempt, its jaw opening to reveal teeth like broken bottles. Rob dived for the cover of trees, some hundred feet below. The Rhampo followed—with its slightly greater bulk and bigger wingspan it began to gain on Rob. He tucked his wings behind him, and fell like an arrow, only leveling out when under the tree canopy. The Rhampo continued to chase through the trees, but Rob was beginning to master his flight controls at last, and threw a quick combination of maneuvers. This was Virtual Reality at its most exciting, and Rob thrilled at every moment. He heard the sound of crashing undergrowth and splintering branches and saw ahead the herd of brachiosaurs. He also noticed for the first time the *Anurognathuses*—identical to his BV—sitting on their backs. As he flew toward them, the teeth of his enemy closed on his wing tip. At the same time, a cluster of *Anurognathus*es rose from the backs of the brachiosaurs and flew straight at him. There was a fearful scream from the *Rhamphorhynchus* as the thirty or more smaller, puffinlike pterosaurs tore at it with their razor-sharp beaks.

Rob landed clumsily upon the back of a brachiosaur and gripped its ridged flesh with his needlelike talons. Rob clicked on his energy level and saw it had dropped to 3.5. He needed rest or food. Or both.

The flock of Anuros flew back with much cawing and croaking. They settled on the rising and falling backs of the Brachios, and scurried over the vast surfaces of rutted skin, pecking with their stubby beaks as they did so. Rob saw to his horror what they were doing, and what he himself would have to do. There were white and bloated ticks the size of small potatoes hanging to the Brachio's skin, hideously long centipedes snaking through the folds of flesh, and bloodsucking flies gorging themselves on the crops of worm-infested wounds around the Brachio's neck. On this repulsive picnic the Anuros were greedily feasting. Rob steeled himself, and did likewise, until his energy level rose a little. Soothed by the sound of the deep rumbling song of his host dinosaur, he closed his eyes and rested.

In real time only a few minutes had passed, but in Virtual Time it had been hours. When he opened his eyes, the forest was in moonlight. He was still on the back of the Brachio, but he had to cling on as the huge animal lurched and rolled. It was plain the Brachio was in trouble. It bellowed and snorted, and lashed its tail. Each time the tail fell, a wall of foul water rose into the air. A chorus of squawks rose into the dark canopy of ancient trees and, as Rob looked over the vast bulk of the Brachio's rump, he saw a marauding pack of *Elaphrosaurus* terrifying the beast. They darted in and nipped its treelike legs with their ferociously sharp teeth. Before the Brachio could react, they had sped away to

A herd of *Brachiosaurus*

a safe distance. Rob understood at once that the *Elaphrosaurus* pack was driving the brachiosaur—either deliberately or by chance—into a swamp. Its many tons of flesh were forcing its huge legs further into the swamp. It was sinking under its own weight, and its death was inescapable. Rob could see the other brachiosaurs standing farther off, rumbling and trumpeting in obvious distress. One of their species was about to meet a slow and untimely end.

Even as Rob flew off the back of the rapidly exhausting brachiosaur, he recognized the menacing shape of a late Jurassic crocodile slide into the waters. In the ghostly electronic moonlight, Rob shuddered with disgust as he heard the brachiosaur roar and hiss with pain, as the crocodile found its mark. Its hunger would soon be satisfied.

The elaphrosaurs, too, had become more daring. They squawked like oversized chickens, and drove the brachiosaur nearer to its doom. Now sunk beyond its knees, it lacked the strength to pull itself from the swamp. Its struggles only forced it farther into the ooze.

Very close to the time limit in DINO, Rob exited with feelings of great sadness for the stricken and helpless beast. As he unhooked the VR harness, he exchanged looks with his sister. Buddy had been following his progress on the monitor, and had seen the sad end of the brachiosaur. She put her arm around Rob as Dr. Harlow quietly explained:

"What you may have witnessed there, Rob, was a species no longer in harmony with its environment. The brachiosaurs needed vast quantities of fuel, and to find it they had to stay constantly on the move. When food got scarce, they had to move to hostile country —like swamps. It was a choice between death by starvation, or death by . . . well, you saw what happened."

"But it was so cruel. It didn't stand a chance," Rob said.

"Animals in the wild are not known for their kindness to each other—even now," Dr. Harlow said, as he closed down the computer.

To cheer him up, Buddy said: "At least you know how to fly by VR now. You were great flying through those trees."

Rob smiled, pleased by the compliment.

"I'm starving," he said, and realized he really was ravenous.

"That's good," Buddy said, "because we're having your favorite supper—boiled ticks and fried centipedes."

GLOSSARY

Brachiosaurids ("arm reptiles"): Giant-sized, four-legged, plant-eating dinosaurs with long necks, deep bodies, heavy legs, and a short, thick tail; includes *Brachiosaurus* and its cousins.

Browser: An animal that feeds on the shoots of bushes and trees.

Carnivore ("meat eater"): An animal that eats other animals.

Community: Plants and animals living together in one area; the animals either feed upon the plants (herbivores), or each other (carnivores).

Conifer: A type of evergreen tree, usually with cones and needlelike leaves.

Continent: A major land mass such as Africa, Europe, or North America.

Coral reef: A small island or reef formed by coral—a small marine invertebrate, usually living in a colony.

Cretaceous ("of the chalk"): The third and final period of the "Age of Dinosaurs" – from 145 to 65 million years ago.

Cycad: A tropical, or subtropical, palmlike plant.

Diplocids ("double beams"): A family of very large and long, four-legged, plant-eating dinosaurs; includes *Diplodocus*, *Barosaurus*, and *Supersaurus*.

Dryosaurids ("oak reptiles"): Small to medium-sized, two-legged, plant-eating dinosaurs; includes *Dryosaurus*.

Gastroliths: Stones that helped a dinosaur's digestive processes by lodging in its gizzard, where they ground plant food into a pulp.

Ginkgo: A primitive tree with fan-shaped leaves, probably eaten by dinosaurs.

Gizzard: A muscular portion of the stomach, where the food is ground up, often with the help of gastroliths (stomach stones).

Herbivore ("plant eater"): An animal that eats plants.

Intestine: A long muscular tube, part of the digestive system, in which food is broken down and absorbed into the body.

Jurassic ("Jura-age," after the Jura Mountains of France, which are made of rocks from this time): The second or middle period of the "Age of Dinosaurs" – from 205 to 145 million years ago.

Mass extinction: The dying out of many different kinds of plants or animals at the same time.

Mesozoic ("middle life"): The whole of the "Age of Dinosaurs," consisting of the Triassic, Jurassic, and Cretaceous periods. It lasted from 245 to 65 million years ago.

Ornithopod ("bird foot"): Small to medium-sized plant-eating dinosaur that could stand on two legs and had a stiff tail; includes *Dryosaurus* and the duckbills.

Paleontologist ("ancient life studier"): A scientist who studies prehistoric life and its fossil evidence.

Predator: A meat-eating animal that hunts and kills other animals for food.

Pterosaur ("wing reptile"): Extinct flying reptiles with wings of skin supported by the greatly enlarged fourth finger.

Sauropod ("reptile foot"): Large to giant-sized, four-footed, plant-eating dinosaur with a long tail and neck, such as *Apatosaurus* or *Brachiosaurus*.

Scavenger: An animal that feeds on either dead or dying animals.

Theropod ("beast foot"): A two-footed meat-eating dinosaur, such as *Ceratosaurus* and *Elaphrosaurus*.

Titanosaurids ("titanic reptiles"): Small to large-sized sauropods that lived from the late Jurassic to the late Cretaceous. They include *Saltasaurus* and *Titantosaurus*.

Trackway: A line of footprints left by an animal walking across soft ground.

INDEX

Page numbers in *italic* refer to the illustrations

KINGFISHER
Larousse Kingfisher Chambers Inc.
95 Madison Avenue
New York, New York 10016

First American edition 1994
2 4 6 8 10 9 7 5 3 1 (lib. bdg.)
2 4 6 8 10 9 7 5 3 (pbk.)

Library of Congress Cataloging-in-Publication Data
Unwin, David.
Brachiosaurus/by David Unin.—1st American ed.
p.   cm.—(Dinoworld)
Includes index.
1. Brachiosaurus—Juvenile literature.   [1. Brachiosaurus.
2. Dinosaurs.]   I. Title   II. Series.
QE862.S3U59 1994
567.9'7—dc20   93–46612 CIP AC

ISBN 1-85697-620-3 (lib. bdg.)
ISBN 1-85697-990-3 (pbk.)

Series Editor: Michèle Byam
Series Designer: Shaun Barlow
Picture Research: Elaine Willis

Dinoventures are written
by Jim Miles

Additional help from Andy Archer, Cathy Tincknell,
Janet Woronkowicz, Matthew Gore, Smiljka Surla, and Hilary Bird

The publishers wish to thank the following artists for
contributing to the book:
Apple Illustrations Agency, Adrian Chesterman (Art Collection), David
Cook (Linden Artists), Eugene Fleury, Chris Forsey, Terry Gabbey (Eva
Morris AFA), Josephine Martin (Garden Studio), Roger Payne (Linden
Artists), Clive Pritchard (Wildlife Art Agency), Luis Rey, Guy Smith
(Mainline Design), Studio Boni Lalli, Studio Galante, Guy Troughton

The publishers wish to thank the following for
supplying photographs for the book:
American Museum of Natural History, neg. no. 125158;
Museum für Naturkinde der Humboldt, Berlin

Printed in Hong Kong

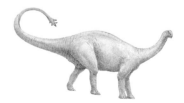